●═ MEETINGS THAT WORK!

A Practical Guide To Shorter And More Productive Meetings

Richard Y. Chang

Kevin R. Kehoe

Jossey-Bass
Pfeiffer
San Francisco

RICHARD
CHANG
ASSOCIATES

ISBN: 0-7879-5079-3

Printed in the United States of America

Published by

350 Sansome Street, 5th Floor
San Francisco, California 94104-1342
(415) 433-1740; Fax (415) 433-0499
(800) 274-4434; Fax (800) 569-0443

Visit our website at: www.pfeiffer.com

Printing   10   9   8   7   6   5   4   3   2   1

ACKNOWLEDGMENTS

About The Authors

Richard Y. Chang, is President and CEO of Richard Chang Associates, Inc., a diversified organizational improvement consulting firm based in Irvine, California. He is internationally recognized for his management strategy, quality improvement, organization development, customer satisfaction, and human resource development expertise.

Kevin R. Kehoe, owner of Kevin Kehoe & Company, is an experienced executive, consultant, and educator. He is widely known and highly regarded for his leadership development, total quality, and reengineering expertise.

The authors would like to acknowledge the support of the entire team of professionals at Richard Chang Associates, Inc. for their contributions to the guidebook development process. In addition, special thanks are extended to the many client organizations who have helped us shape the practical ideas and proven methods shared in this guidebook.

Additional Credits

Editor:	Sarah Ortlieb Fraser
Reviewers:	P. Keith Kelly, Benjamin Krepack, and Ruth Stingley
Graphic Layout:	Christina Slater
Cover Design:	John Odam Design Associates

PREFACE

The 1990's have already presented individuals and organizations with some very difficult challenges to face and overcome. So who will have the advantage as we move toward the year 2000 and beyond?

The advantage will belong to those with a commitment to continuous learning. Whether on an individual basis or as an entire organization, one key ingredient to building a continuous learning environment is *The Practical Guidebook Collection* brought to you by the Publications Division of Richard Chang Associates, Inc.

After understanding the future *"learning needs"* expressed by our clients and other potential customers, we are pleased to publish *The Practical Guidebook Collection*. These guidebooks are designed to provide you with proven, *"real-world"* tips, tools, and techniques—on a wide range of subjects—that you can apply in the workplace and/or on a personal level immediately.

Once you've had a chance to benefit from *The Practical Guidebook Collection*, please share your feedback with us. We've included a brief *Evaluation and Feedback Form* at the end of the guidebook that you can fax to us at (714) 727-7007.

With your feedback, we can continuously improve the resources we are providing through the Publications Division of Richard Chang Associates, Inc.

Wishing you successful reading,

Richard Y. Chang
President and CEO
Richard Chang Associates, Inc.

TABLE OF CONTENTS

One perception of meetings...

Two managers talking:

Ed: *"Let's cut out the staff meetings."*
Pam: *"We can't. I need the sleep!"*

and another...

*"Nothing more effectively involves people,
sustains creditability, or generates
enthusiasm than face-to-face
communication."*

Dana Corporation philosophy

and yet another...

*"If managers spend more than 25 percent of
their time in meetings, it is a sign of poor
organization."*

Peter F. Drucker

CHAPTER ONE

INTRODUCTION

Webster's Dictionary defines the word *"meeting"* as *"an act or process of coming together; an assembly for a common purpose."* The key word in this definition is *"process."* Without an organized game plan, a meeting may become a time-consuming discussion among a group of individuals.

A poorly planned meeting often results in mixed messages among participants, unclear goals and strategies, and a random list of things to be done afterwards. Unfortunately, the lack of results at one meeting usually leads to yet another time-consuming, non-productive meeting.

Why Read This Guidebook?

What's the solution? Do we rely solely on written memos, electronic mail, and one-on-one communication? And should we do away with meetings altogether and change conference rooms into paddleball courts and child day-care centers?

The answer, of course, is no. Meetings are here to stay. From the beginning of time, face-to-face gatherings of people, or meetings, have been used by men and women to exchange ideas, information, and knowledge.

Whether to simply share information in staff meetings, solve problems with a group of people, work on a quality-improvement team, or focus task-force efforts, productive meetings can offer a number of benefits to you and your fellow participants. These benefits include, but are not limited to:

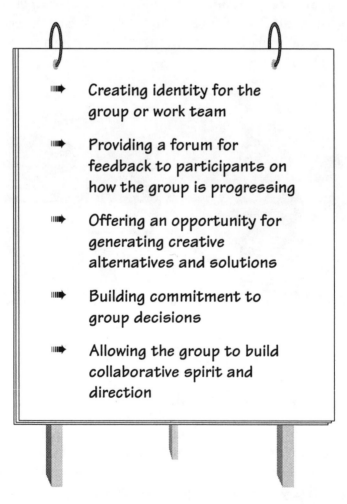

- Creating identity for the group or work team

- Providing a forum for feedback to participants on how the group is progressing

- Offering an opportunity for generating creative alternatives and solutions

- Building commitment to group decisions

- Allowing the group to build collaborative spirit and direction

Over the years, businesses and organizations have adopted a set format for meetings. That format may no longer be as effective today as it once was. And with the increasing emphasis on improving productivity, you should seriously consider the opportunity to improve the format of business meetings. A meeting can be thought of as a *"process,"* like other workplace processes, with plenty of room for improvement.

The meeting process, when conducted well, can encourage more team involvement and provide a way for all involved to feel they are playing a key role in a team effort.

This guidebook provides theory, concepts, and tools for participating in such a process. It is easy to understand and use. You'll find examples of all the forms you need. After reading this guidebook, you'll be able to accomplish more in your meetings!

Who Should Read This Guidebook?

Anyone in an organization who plans, runs, or attends meetings can benefit from the tips and techniques presented in this guidebook. Whether you are in a managerial position supervising others, part of a work team, a sales representative, a trainer, an accountant, a programmer, or an engineer, meetings are a normal part of the work environment. Everyone who participates in any kind of meeting can use the ideas and tools presented in this guidebook to achieve better meeting results.

When And How To Use It

Use this guidebook, or selected ideas from it, to help improve your regular staff, project, or quality team meetings, as well as meetings that are not regularly scheduled. Share key points with others, and most importantly, *try* these ideas. Regular practice is the key to successful meetings.

MAKING MEETINGS WORK

Take a look around your work area and notice the doorways, walls, and floor coverings. Behind and beneath them are wires, pipes, and cables you can't see, and perhaps there is a window with a view. What does it take to build a structure like this? The answer is planning, managing, and problem solving by key players.

▼

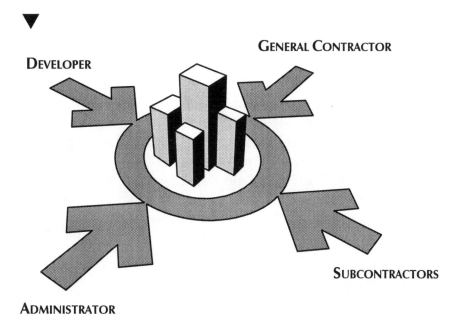

GENERAL CONTRACTOR

DEVELOPER

SUBCONTRACTORS

ADMINISTRATOR

First of all, a Developer oversees the entire project. He or she understands the big picture, is responsible for successfully *(or unsuccessfully)* completing the building, and has the authority to *"call the shots"* while the building is being constructed.

▶

DEVELOPER

But the developer can't do it all alone. He or she relies on a General Contractor to manage the project and fix problems. These responsibilities include managing the activities of others on the project, particularly Subcontractors such as plumbers and electricians, and depending on each of them for their special skills and knowledge.

GENERAL CONTRACTOR

The team also depends on an Administrator, who keeps track of the project, including the visual picture, or blueprint, of the building. The Administrator makes sure each person knows what needs to be accomplished, and how to work with the others to get the job done.

ADMINISTRATOR

Finally, there are the Subcontractors, or front-line team members, who get the work done. They report to the General Contractor on the project's problems and progress.

SUBCONTRACTOR

These four key players and the roles they play in constructing a building have counterparts in meetings. Just as the key players in construction ensure the building is finished on time and within budget, similar key players have specific roles during the meeting process.

The Four Meeting Roles

Let's take a closer look at four key meeting roles and how they contribute to conducting more effective and productive meetings.

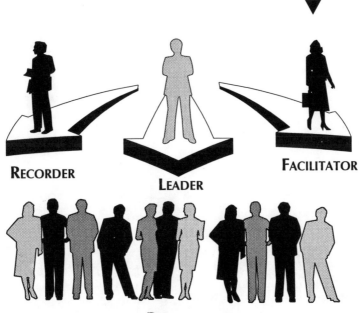

RECORDER

LEADER

FACILITATOR

PARTICIPANTS

LEADER ▶ The Leader of the meeting *(playing a role similar to the Developer)* establishes the meeting objectives and plans, and is responsible for the overall direction of the meeting.

FACILITATOR ▶ The Leader depends on the Facilitator *(playing a role similar to the General Contractor)* to manage how people work together in the meeting. The Facilitator also helps Participants clear up conflicts and solve problems quickly to keep the meeting moving along.

RECORDER ► The Recorder *(playing a role similar to the Administrator)* is responsible for keeping track of the vital information from the meeting and keeping it visual. The Recorder also makes sure the information is accurate, and helps to distribute it among Participants.

Agenda

Introduction of agenda

Generate a list

Develop criteria

Apply criteria

PARTICIPANTS

▶ The Participants *(playing a role similar to the Subcontractors)*, a group of individuals with a variety of skills, talents, and personalities, are part of the meeting team. They are responsible for getting the job done. Participants generate ideas, analyze information, make decisions, and implement action plans.

You're on the right track toward getting the most out of your meetings once all of your meeting Participants understand these roles during each meeting. Keep reading to learn more about the roles and how to play them.

CHAPTER TWO WORKSHEET:
ROLES FOR YOUR MEETINGS

1. What formal roles do you use for your meetings?

_____

_____

_____

_____

_____

_____

2. What are the biggest challenges faced by each of these roles?

_____

_____

_____

_____

_____

_____

_____

_____

_____

3. At this point, what changes would you consider making in the roles to have more effective meetings?

_____

_____

_____

_____

_____

_____

_____

_____

_____

_____

_____

_____

_____

_____

_____

THREE ESSENTIAL MEETING STAGES

A successful and productive meeting requires more than just clear role definition, it needs a basic structure. Without a structure, several people will come together with different ideas about what is going to happen, when and how it is going to happen, and who is supposed to make it happen.

Have you experienced meetings that turned into long-winded get-togethers, where nothing was accomplished? This can easily happen unless meetings are conducted with a structure everyone knows and follows.

A basic meeting structure that has proven helpful in overcoming these potential meeting pitfalls includes the following three essential stages:

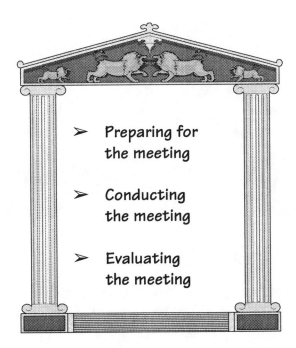

➤ **Preparing for the meeting**

➤ **Conducting the meeting**

➤ **Evaluating the meeting**

Preparing For The Meeting

One of the keys to a successful meeting can be found in the upcoming chapter. You will read about planning, preparation, and the *"legwork"*—such as creating an agenda—that is required before Participants enter the meeting room's door.

Conducting The Meeting

In meetings, attendees generate ideas, make decisions, and ask questions. A well-conducted meeting provides an effective forum for accomplishing meeting objectives. Chapter Five describes the roles people should play at meetings, what their responsibilities are, and tips for keeping meetings productive and on track.

Evaluating The Meeting

Improvement comes with evaluating what we do, using effective techniques, searching for areas to improve, and making necessary changes. With meetings being such an important part of life in an organization, it is critical to improve your meeting process. Chapter Six presents techniques and tools for evaluating and improving your meetings.

On the following pages, we will look at the *"nuts and bolts"* of these three essential stages, explaining what to do during each stage and how to do it.

CHAPTER THREE WORKSHEET: ROLES FOR YOUR MEETINGS

1. What problems, or areas for improvement, have you encountered with your meetings, at the following stages? What might you do to solve the problems and improve your meetings?

    a. Preparing for the meeting.

PROBLEMS/AREAS FOR IMPROVEMENT	SOLUTIONS/IMPROVEMENT IDEAS

    b. Conducting the meeting.

PROBLEMS/AREAS FOR IMPROVEMENT	SOLUTIONS/IMPROVEMENT IDEAS

    c. Evaluating the meeting.

PROBLEMS/AREAS FOR IMPROVEMENT	SOLUTIONS/IMPROVEMENT IDEAS

2. Which of these phases offers the greatest opportunity for improvement?

_____

_____

_____

_____

_____

3. What can you do to make improvements *(be specific)*?

    a. In the short run? *(For your next meeting.)*

_____

_____

_____

_____

_____

    b. In the long run?

_____

_____

_____

_____

_____

PREPARING FOR THE MEETING

Asked why they find meetings unproductive or frustrating, people often respond with comments such as:

"Nobody was clear on what the meeting objective was, or what we were supposed to do next."

"With only a few hours notice, people will come half prepared, at best."

"The Participants didn't know they were supposed to bring reports or materials."

"The people invited to attend didn't know why they were supposed to be there."

When it comes to meetings, the expression, *"an ounce of prevention is worth a pound of cure,"* rings true. An hour or two of preparation can save several hours spent in meetings each month. Each and every person involved in the meeting has an important role to play in preparing for it. Just showing up isn't enough—not if you are serious about making your meetings more productive!

Responsibilities Before The Meeting

The meeting roles introduced earlier—those of Leader, Facilitator, Recorder, and Participants—include responsibilities that begin before the meeting starts. These responsibilities are:

LEADER

- Schedules meeting
- Prepares the agenda
- Clarifies Participants' roles and responsibilities

FACILITATOR

- Reviews agenda and action plans from previous meeting
- Completes any necessary preparation
- Works with Leader on logistics

RECORDER

- Reviews agenda and action plans from previous meeting
- Completes any necessary preparation

PARTICIPANTS

- Review agenda and action plans from previous meeting
- Complete any necessary preparation

The person who plays the biggest role in preparing for the meeting is the Leader, who essentially *"owns"* the meeting at this stage and is getting other people to *"buy in"* to their roles. As you can see from the responsibilities listed above, the common thread running through each of the roles is the agenda, the most important tool in preparing for a successful and productive meeting.

Using A Meeting Agenda

Just as the developer works from a blueprint and shares it with other people working on the building, a meeting should have a *"blueprint"* the Leader can share with Participants.

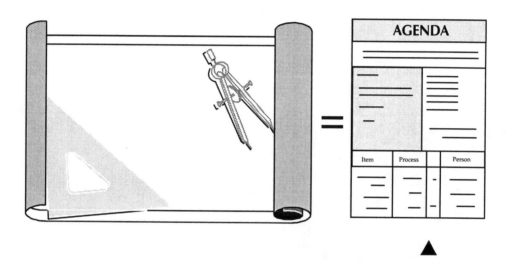

The blueprint for any meeting is its agenda, which provides everyone with a picture of what the meeting will look like.

Why have an agenda? Well, can you imagine trying to build a building without a blueprint? Where would you start? How long would it take? Who would do what, and when? The blueprint is the starting point to answer these questions.

The agenda covers the big picture and lays out enough information so all Participants know what their roles are. Just like the building blueprint used by the developer, the agenda is the tool the meeting Leader prepares and uses to show what has to be accomplished by the Participants, and in what order.

A written agenda, prepared and circulated at least two days in advance of a meeting, helps protect against the types of post-meeting comments previously described. Below is one type of agenda.

MEETING AGENDA

MEETING OBJECTIVE(S):

1._____

2. _____

3. _____

LOGISTICS:	GROUP MEMBERS:	
DATE:	1. _____	(LEADER)
TIME:	2. _____	(FACILITATOR)
LOCATION:	3. _____	(RECORDER)
BRING (MATERIALS):	4. _____	
	5. _____	
	6. _____	
PREPARATION REQUIRED:	7. _____	
	8. _____	
	MEETING CALLED BY: _____	
	TELEPHONE: _____	

AGENDA ITEM	PROCESS	TIME	PERSON(S) RESPONSIBLE

Much of the responsibility for developing the agenda lies with the meeting Leader, who also ensures that everyone comes to the meeting prepared.

Members of a customer service department...

wanted to address problems raised in a customer satisfaction survey. Penny, the team leader, decided that the most effective way was to call a meeting of representatives of the customer service department. She quickly realized that they would need to build an agenda....

Building The Agenda

When developing the agenda, it's helpful to follow these five basic steps:

Agenda Steps

Step 1: Establish objective(s)

Step 2: Confirm the logistics

Step 3: Determine the attendees

Step 4: Assign the roles

Step 5: Build the action section of
the agenda

Let's take a closer look at each of the basic steps to developing a useful meeting agenda.

Step 1: Establish The Objective(s)

The first step in preparing an agenda is to establish the objective(s) for the meeting. To do this, the question you have to ask yourself is, *"Why is this meeting necessary?"* Can the objective(s) be accomplished without a meeting?

To help ensure that your meetings are productive, don't attempt to hold a meeting when:

➠ The appropriate Participants are not all available

➠ There is not enough time to go over the subject properly, or too much detail to remember

➠ There is inadequate data or time to prepare

➠ The subject is so confidential (e.g., sensitive personnel issues), it can't be completely shared with other Participants

➠ Your mind is made up—you have already made your decision

➠ The subject is trivial

➠ There is too much hostility in the group—people need time to calm down before they begin to work collaboratively toward the meeting objective(s)

➠ The subject matter could be addressed more effectively through other means or methods

Penny sought input in establishing the objectives...

by asking others, *"We have this disappointing data from the customer satisfaction survey, now what do we do to address the problems raised?"*

Based on the group's input, Penny decided that the objective of their meeting would be to select three possible solutions to address problems raised in the customer satisfaction survey....

Once the need for a meeting is confirmed, the Leader needs to spell out the objective. In other words, answer the question, *"What is the desired outcome from this meeting?"* It should be brief, concise, and written as a goal *(or goals)*, rather than as a vague statement.

Avoid phrases such as *"discuss the new accounts payable system"* or *"talk about the recent training effort."* Instead, be specific and use action words *(e.g., assign, decide, determine, create, complete, and produce.)*

Here are a few examples of goal-oriented meeting objectives:

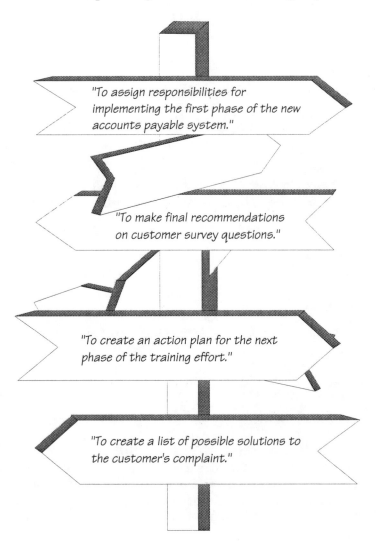

"To assign responsibilities for implementing the first phase of the new accounts payable system."

"To make final recommendations on customer survey questions."

"To create an action plan for the next phase of the training effort."

"To create a list of possible solutions to the customer's complaint."

Remember the objective of Penny's customer service department? Like those listed on the previous page, it is clear and straightforward. Everyone will know exactly what he or she is trying to accomplish in the meeting.

MEETING AGENDA
MEETING OBJECTIVE(S):
1. <u>To select three possible solutions to address problems raised in the customer</u> <u>satisfaction survey.</u>

Have your own meeting objectives been this clear? Notice, this objective is written as a specific, tangible goal to work toward during the meeting.

Step 2: Confirm The Logistics

Everyone needs detailed information about the when, where, what, and who of the meeting. Thus, it is important to be specific about the date, time, location, and materials the Participants should bring to the meeting *(e.g., memos, reports, documents, samples, organizational charts, etc.)*, and any special preparation or reading required.

LOGISTICS:
DATE: April 20 19XX
TIME: 10:00 A.M. to 10:45 A.M.
LOCATION: Room 404
BRING (MATERIALS):
Agenda and customer satisfaction survey reports

PREPARATION REQUIRED:
Review survey reports

This information helps you avoid wasting valuable time at the beginning of the meeting to bring Participants *"up to speed"* about specific facts and events.

Penny felt that the size of the meeting...

should be the most important factor in choosing a meeting site. Room 404 on the fourth floor would hold 12 people. Since there were eight to ten people from customer service department scheduled for Penny's meeting, she chose that room. The time most convenient for everyone was 10 A.M. the following Monday....

Where you hold a meeting can influence how the meeting runs. While the right room can't guarantee a good meeting, an inappropriate room can create a disaster!

Additional meeting logistics to consider

No matter how important your meeting is, it still may be non-productive when distractions are present. Consider each of the following elements when preparing for a meeting.

ELEMENTS	CONSIDERATIONS
Room Arrangements	Type of meeting; convenient location; appropriate size; privacy; freedom from distractions; flow of information, etc.
Seating Arrangements	Adequate number of chairs; appropriate arrangement of tables/chairs to meet desired degree of participation; no obstructions of view; available writing surfaces, etc.
Lighting	Ability to regulate for slides and overhead transparencies; adequate for note taking, etc.
Ventilation	Ability to regulate *(especially for all-day meetings)*; smoking/nonsmoking areas, etc.
Audio/visual	Slide projector; video monitor and deck; overhead projector; flip chart pad(s) and stand(s); computer terminals, etc.
Miscellaneous Support	Adequate handouts; pencils; paper; parking validations, etc.
Refreshments	Adequate coffee breaks; snacks; meals; catering service, etc.
People	Resource people *"on stand-by,"* catering, audio/visual and computer specialists; conference room coordinator, etc.

Step 3: Determine The Attendees

The Leader determines and writes on the agenda the list of who should attend the meeting. After all, why have people at a meeting who neither need nor want to be there? People have other demands on their time.

GROUP MEMBERS:
1. Penny
2. Paul
3. Joe
4. Christina
5. Anthony
6. Matt
7. Larry
8. Donna

MEETING CALLED BY: Penny
TELEPHONE: ext. 227

Agenda Step 3 also reinforces the need to establish goal-oriented meeting objectives. Without specific objective(s), it isn't clear who needs to attend the meeting.

People who should be invited include:

→ Subject-matter experts

→ Key decision makers

→ Those whose jobs are directly affected by the objective(s) of the meeting

Those who should not be invited include:

→ People who are unaffected by the objective(s) of the meeting

→ Known meeting *"disrupters"*

→ Those whose feelings may be hurt if they are left out

Who is invited is as important as what you are meeting about. The nonparticipants may still contribute to the meeting by providing input for agenda items, and they can receive the meeting minutes. You may find that many people actually appreciate not being invited to a meeting.

In deciding who should attend...

the meeting, Penny kept in mind those who were most affected by the problems raised in the customer satisfaction survey. She decided to include three people from customer relations, a supervisor in the customer support area, and three front-line customer relations people *(because they deal with customers all the time)....*

Step 4: Assign The Roles

Let's go back for a moment to our analogy comparing meetings to the construction of a building. The Leader *(like the developer)* spearheads the effort to bring people together for a specific purpose. But, as any developer knows, it takes general contractors, administrators, and subcontractors to make it all work well.

GROUP MEMBERS:
1. _Penny_ (LEADER)
2. _Paul_ (FACILITATOR)
3. _Joe_ (RECORDER)

The meeting roles:

➠ Give the meeting more structure

➠ Allow everyone to focus on reaching the objective(s) in the time allotted

➠ Should be assigned before the agenda is sent out

➠ Should be rotated depending on the type and frequency of the meetings *(a weekly staff meeting, for example, is a good time to try this)*

No matter how the roles are assigned, it's important to notify the Facilitator and Recorder in advance so they'll know before the meeting what is expected of them.

Paul, from customer relations,...

was chosen as a Facilitator because he'd proven he could keep meetings moving. Penny was the natural choice for Leader. To make things easy, Joe volunteered to be the Recorder....

Step 5: Build The Action Section Of The Agenda

List agenda items

AGENDA ITEM	PROCESS	TIME	PERSON(S) RESPONSIBLE
1) Introduction of agenda			
2) Generate a list			
3) Develop criteria			
4) Apply criteria			

Now it's time to identify a list of items that will be necessary to achieve your meeting's objective(s). Agenda items are first developed by the Leader, with suggestions and input from the people who will be participating.

The agenda should be clear, using familiar terms and phrases. Abbreviations and acronyms should be avoided if they are not known by all Participants.

Agenda items can be sequenced in a number of ways, depending on the situation. For example, you can list the items according to importance, urgency, potential for conflict, or in logical order. A magic recipe does not exist.

Here are a few tips for sequencing agenda items effectively:

☛ Start with the most important items, allowing the Participants to make critical decisions when their interest and energy are at their highest levels.

☛ Handle short, urgent items first so they aren't crowded out and become continuous *"old business"* items.

☛ Concentrate on fewer, more important items.

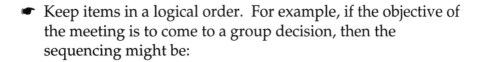

☛ Keep items in a logical order. For example, if the objective of the meeting is to come to a group decision, then the sequencing might be:

1. Define the problem

2. Evaluate solutions

3. Vote on the best solutions

4. Assign responsibilities

> ## "It's time to identify a list of items...
> *that will be necessary to achieve our meeting's objective,"* thought Penny. She determined that the agenda items would be the following: introduction of agenda, generate a list, develop criteria, and apply criteria. She asked for everyone's input in building the agenda items....

Establish the process for each item

▼

AGENDA ITEM	PROCESS	TIME	PERSON(S) RESPONSIBLE
1) Introduction of agenda	Presentation		
2) Generate a list	Brainstorming sessions in 2 groups		
3) Develop criteria	Brainstorming session—entire group		
4) Apply criteria	Decision		

Choosing a process for each agenda item means selecting a method to *"tackle"* each topic listed.

Some examples of processes you might use include:

- ◆ Discussion
- ◆ Brainstorming session
- ◆ Presentation

- ◆ Vote
- ◆ Consensus building
- ◆ Decision

Time for each item ⟶

AGENDA ITEM	PROCESS	TIME	PERSON(S) RESPONSIBLE
1) Introduction of agenda	Presentation	5 min	
2) Generate a list	Brainstorming sessions in 2 groups	15 min	
3) Develop criteria	Brainstorming session—entire group	10 min	
4) Apply criteria	Decision	15 min	

◀ As you have probably experienced, it's common to try to accomplish too much in a single meeting. Part of your role is to use this agenda as a tool to keep your meeting on target.

Being unrealistic about the time it takes to discuss something might mean some agenda items won't be covered or the meeting may last longer than intended, which no one wants.

Note that the sample agenda has specific times allocated for each of the four items, ranging from 5 minutes for the introduction to 15 minutes for items 2 and 4.

Identify person(s) responsible

AGENDA ITEM	PROCESS	TIME	PERSON(S) RESPONSIBLE
1) Introduction of agenda	Presentation	5 min	Penny
2) Generate a list	Brainstorming sessions in 2 groups	15 min	Christina, Anthony
3) Develop criteria	Brainstorming session—entire group	10 min	Matt
4) Apply criteria	Decision	15 min	Larry

If different people are responsible for certain parts of the meeting, the agenda should show who is handling each item. This way, there is no confusion. Everyone knows who "has the floor" for a given topic, and for how long.

Depending on the item, it may be a good idea to have a subject-matter expert on the topic report first to get the discussion rolling. Also, if all Participants are given responsibilities, it fosters a feeling that everyone plays a key role and is part of the "real team."

Here's the complete meeting agenda that Penny built with input from other members of the customer service department.

MEETING AGENDA			

MEETING OBJECTIVE(S):

1. <u>To select three possible solutions to address problems raised in the customer satisfaction survey.</u>

2. _____

3. _____

LOGISTICS:

DATE: April 20 19XX

TIME: 10:00 a.m. to 10:45 a.m.

LOCATION: Room 404

BRING (MATERIALS):
Agenda and customer satisfaction
survey results reports

PREPARATION REQUIRED:
Review results reports

GROUP MEMBERS:

1. <u>Penny</u> (LEADER)

2. <u>Paul</u> (FACILITATOR)

3. <u>Joe</u> (RECORDER)

4. <u>Christina</u>

5. <u>Anthony</u>

6. <u>Matt</u>

7. <u>Larry</u>

8. <u>Donna</u>

MEETING CALLED BY: <u>Penny</u>

TELEPHONE: <u>ext. 227</u>

AGENDA ITEM	PROCESS	TIME	PERSON(S) RESPONSIBLE
1) Introduction of agenda and ground rules	Presentation	5 min	Penny
2) Generate a list of solutions based on customer satisfaction survey	Brainstorming sessions in 2 groups	15 min	Christina, Anthony
3) Develop criteria for selecting the three best solutions	Brainstorming session—entire group	10 min	Matt
4) Apply criteria and select the three best solutions	Decision	15 min	Larry

CHAPTER FOUR WORKSHEET: PREPARING FOR YOUR NEXT MEETING

1. What key objective do you want to accomplish in your next meeting?

_____

_____

_____

_____

2a. How long should the meeting be and when should it be held?

_____

_____

_____

_____

2b. What materials/information will Participants need to bring? What should they prepare in advance?

_____

_____

_____

_____

_____

3. Who really needs to be present? Include those with decision-making authority, those whose commitment and support are needed, and those who need to be kept informed.

NAME	REASON INVITED
_____	_____
_____	_____
_____	_____
_____	_____
_____	_____
_____	_____
_____	_____
_____	_____
_____	_____
_____	_____
_____	_____
_____	_____

4. Who will be the Leader? Facilitator? Recorder?

LEADER	FACILITATOR	RECORDER
_____	_____	_____

5. What items/topics need to be addressed? What meeting
process will be used, by whom, and for how long?

AGENDA ITEM	PROCESS	WHOM	TIME FRAME
_____	_____	_____	_____
_____	_____	_____	_____
_____	_____	_____	_____
_____	_____	_____	_____
_____	_____	_____	_____
_____	_____	_____	_____
_____	_____	_____	_____
_____	_____	_____	_____

6. Additional meeting preparation notes:

_____

_____

_____

_____

_____

_____

_____

_____

_____

CONDUCTING THE MEETING

It's time to conduct your meeting. We've discussed why we need to improve on the meeting process and we've taken the time to prepare for what's ahead. Let's now take a look at each of the four roles, define their key responsibilities, and describe the way each contributes to the success of the meeting.

LEADER

♦ Starts the meeting on time

♦ Clarifies roles

♦ Establishes ground rules and guidelines

♦ Participates as a group member

♦ Follows the agenda

♦ Retains the power to stop what's happening and change the format

♦ Pushes for accountability

♦ Summarizes key decisions and actions

FACILITATOR

♦ Focuses the group on the same issue

♦ Ensures participation from everyone

♦ Regulates discussion "traffic"

♦ Monitors time spent on each agenda item

♦ Suggests alternate methods and processes

♦ Protects people and their ideas from attack

♦ Deals with problem people

♦ Remains neutral during disagreements

RECORDER

♦ Captures ideas visually without editing or paraphrasing

♦ Regularly checks to ensure appropriate information has been recorded

♦ Helps the Leader and Facilitator keep track of information

♦ Produces the meeting minutes

PARTICIPANTS

♦ Know the purpose of the meeting ahead of time

♦ Confirm attendance

♦ Attend meeting on time

♦ Keep an open mind and avoid premature judgement

♦ Helps the Facilitator eliminate distractions and encourage active involvement

♦ Share useful ideas

♦ Support established ground rules and meeting guidelines

♦ Help to ensure group consensus

The Leader's Role

Specifically, the Leader:

➠ Starts the meeting on time

One of the most widespread complaints about meetings is waiting for stragglers to show up. The Leader has the authority and the responsibility to start at the scheduled time. If the Leader makes a habit of starting on time, others will show up promptly.

➠ Clarifies roles

The Leader should review and explain to the members of the group what their meeting roles and responsibilities are.

➠ Establishes ground rules and guidelines

Without ground rules, everyone in a meeting has a different idea of what's acceptable and what's not. These rules should be made clear to everyone.

> **GROUND RULES**
>
> ○ Don't interrupt when another Participant "has the floor."
>
> ○ Don't criticize the ideas of others.
>
> ○ Build on the ideas shared by others.
>
> ○ Remain open-minded and nonjudgemental.
>
> ○ Start and end the meeting on time.
>
> ○ Everyone participates, no one dominates.
>
> ○ Complaints are okay when they come packaged with a solution.
>
> ○ Make compromises when necessary.
>
> ○ The Facilitator is empowered to enforce ground rules.
>
> ○ Stick to the Agenda and time frames.

➠ Participates as a group member

The Leader can add special insights that may help a group reach its objective. The Leader has a responsibility to participate just like everyone else.

⇒ Follows the agenda

The Leader has a special responsibility as the *"owner"* of the meeting to make sure he or she keeps it on track by following the agenda.

⇒ Retains the power to stop what's happening and change the format

Even though the Facilitator is responsible for the meeting process, the Leader can step in and change things if necessary, to get back on track to reaching the meeting's objective(s).

⇒ Pushes for accountability

The Leader has the authority to push when necessary to get things done. He or she may, for example, assign tasks and additional responsibilities to Participants in order to hold them accountable.

⇒ Summarizes key decisions and actions

As part of the content responsibility, the Leader has to make sure decisions and actions are clearly understood and that they are moving in the right direction to accomplish the meeting objective(s).

Penny called the meeting...

to order. She reviewed meeting roles with the group. Again, Paul was the Facilitator and Joe was the Recorder. Penny led the group through a discussion of establishing ground rules and guidelines for how the group would function during the meeting. *"Are there any additions to the meeting agenda?"* asked Penny. *"If there are, we need to decide whether there is enough time to cover the items and if something else needs to be taken out of the agenda."*

Penny proceeded with each item on the agenda. She covered the person(s) responsible for each item, the time allotted, and the process the group would use for each item. As the meeting continued, Penny actively participated and made sure that tasks discussed were assigned to individuals....

The Facilitator's Role

Since the Leader is responsible for managing the agenda, someone else has to keep time and manage the *"people side"* of what happens. The Facilitator has to act as a combination of traffic cop, referee, and timekeeper during the meeting. Specifically, the Facilitator:

▼

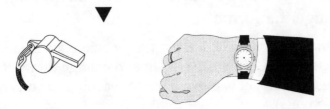

➠ Focuses the group on the same issue

The Facilitator has to make sure the group stays focused on the issues at hand. He or she may actually have to interrupt and remind people of what they are trying to accomplish.

➠ Ensures participation from everyone

Some people are quiet by nature. The Facilitator includes everyone, so that valuable contributions do not go unspoken.

➠ Regulates discussion *"traffic"*

This can be one of the Facilitator's toughest jobs—managing the verbal behaviors of people, such as knowing when to tell an individual to give up the floor, discouraging Participants from talking all at once, and so on.

➠ Monitors time spent on each agenda item

It is the Facilitator's responsibility to let the Participants know when they have spent the assigned amount of time on an agenda item. He or she can then ask the Participants whether they wish to add more time, handle the issue outside of the meeting, or move to the next agenda item.

➠ Suggests alternate methods and processes

When the process indicated on the agenda isn't working, the Facilitator should point this out to the group and help them agree on another approach.

➠ Protects people and their ideas from attack

Nobody should take it personally when the Facilitator steps in to calm a situation. After all, the Facilitator is, by definition, empowered to handle people and problems in the meeting.

➠ Deals with problem people

Chances are you have been frustrated at meetings with problem people, especially when no one does anything about them. It's in these types of situations that a Facilitator can play an important role. See Appendix A—Common Problems And Solutions For Meeting Facilitators to give you some workable ideas.

➠ Remains neutral during disagreements

Someone has to be the arbitrator to step in when there is disagreement. The Facilitator is in a better position to do this than the Leader, since the Leader is not a neutral observer. The Facilitator stays focused on the process.

Paul ensured that each person...

in the meeting got an opportunity to discuss the issues as they were presented. When Christina and Anthony were brainstorming, Paul made sure that all of the team members had an opportunity to provide input. He also ensured that all of the Participants stuck to the agenda's time frame. At one point, Paul had to tell Larry and Donna to focus back on the agenda because they were engaging in a side conversation....

More On The Facilitator's Role

What is the difference between a Facilitator and a Leader? The Leader is driving, or focusing on, the content of the meeting, whereas the Facilitator is managing the process of what goes on during the meeting. The Leader is allowed to have an opinion; the Facilitator must remain neutral.

You may be wondering if it's really necessary to have two separate people playing the role of Leader and Facilitator. After all, we've all seen many meetings run by one person, why have two? The answer is simple. It works! Research reveals that in meetings where the two roles have been separated, the results are better. Meetings are shorter by an average of 20 percent, more productive, and require fewer follow-up meetings.

After two or three meetings conducted with both a Leader and a Facilitator, you will notice a difference. Your meetings will be more focused.

On some occasions, it may be necessary to bring in an outside Facilitator. This is because an outside Facilitator can be an objective referee, and not opinionated about meeting items and decisions.

Is there a need for two people to play these roles in a small group? Experience has proven this approach to be beneficial in any meeting of more than four people. Experiment and see how it works!

The Recorder's Role

The Recorder plays an important role during the meeting. In any situation when a lot of information is exchanged, there may be several different interpretations. If, for example, fifteen people witness an auto accident, it's likely there will be fifteen different versions of what occurred. It's not that anyone's story is wrong; each person will explain the experience through his or her own point of view, relating a different story than that of another witness. The same thing can happen with meetings.

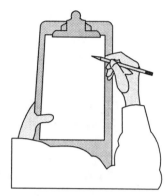

Specifically, the Recorder:

- Penny called the meeting on time

  Introduction to agenda

  Brainstorming session

- Customer satisfaction ideas
  - Lower prices
  - Higher quality
  - Provide better customer service

➠ **Captures ideas visually without editing or paraphrasing**

Ideally, the Recorder will have a flip chart or whiteboard to keep a *"real time"* summary. As the meeting progresses, the Recorder creates a visual blueprint of the discussion, using brief words, phrases, and symbols.

Why a visual record? The simple answer is that our communication and understanding is enhanced when we use visuals. Did you ever wonder why large corporations spend so much money on logos to represent their corporate identities? It's because people remember images and pictures much more clearly than they remember spoken words.

➡ **Regularly checks to ensure appropriate information has been recorded**

The Recorder can be expected to interrupt from time to time to make sure that what he or she wrote down is truly what has been said or decided.

➡ **Helps the Leader and Facilitator keep track of information**

The Leader and Facilitator are focused on where the content and process are going from one minute to the next. They need the Recorder to keep track of the ground that's already been covered and decisions made to date.

➡ **Produces the meeting minutes**

Minutes only need to capture the key decisions and items. If the Recorder follows this rule, you'll find you may not need to go to as many meetings—reading the minutes will provide you with the important information!

Like the Facilitator, the Recorder needs to be trained to have the confidence and the competence to do a good job. When the discussion and ideas are *"flying,"* knowing what to record and what to ignore is important to the success of the meeting.

Joe made sure he recorded...

all of the input and action items along with the names of person(s) who were to be responsible for them. For example, Matt would take the three solutions to senior management for approval, Donna would discuss the solutions with other members of the customer service department and Joe agreed to send the minutes out to the group within a week....

The following list provides some tips and techniques for being an effective Recorder.

✔ Ask for clarification when you need to make sure you have the right information

✔ Write only the key words and phrases. You don't need to get every word, like a court stenographer

✔ Try to use the words expressed, not your own interpretation

✔ Write legibly (print about 2-3" high) on a flip chart or whiteboard, in full view of meeting Participants

✔ Circle or underline key ideas, phrases, decisions, or action items

✔ Number all charts to help maintain order and flow of information

✔ Don't eliminate ideas or phrases just because you don't agree

✔ If the meeting is long and technical, have the group review recorded notes periodically

Here is a sample of the minutes from Penny's customer service department.

MEETING MINUTES			
Meeting Objective(s): To select three possible solutions to address problems raised in the customer satisfaction survey.			
Leader: _Penny_ Facilitator: _Paul_ Recorder: _Joe_		Meeting Called By: _Penny_ Time: From _10:00 AM_ To _10:45 AM_ Date: _April 20, 19XX_	
Members Present: 1. Christina 2. Anthony 3. Matt 4. Larry 5. Donna		**Members Absent:** 1. Hooray! Everyone here! 2. 3. 4. 5.	
AGENDA ITEM	**COMMENTS/ CONCLUSIONS/ ACTIONS (IF ANY)**	**PERSON(S) RESPONSIBLE**	**BY WHEN**
2) Generate a list of solutions based on customer satisfaction survey	The top 20 we agreed on were "keepers": ❑ Develop customer satisfaction criteria ❑ Make more sales calls ❑ Provide more rebates ❑ Provide exclusive territories ❑ Determine customers' future plans/needs ❑ Put customers in an "A" and a "B" group ❑ Devise "tighter" sales plans/goals ❑ Provide training to customers' employees ❑ Etc.		

MEETING MINUTES (CONT.)			
AGENDA ITEM	COMMENTS/ CONCLUSIONS/ ACTIONS (IF ANY)	PERSON(S) RESPONSIBLE	BY WHEN
3) Develop criteria for selecting the three best solutions	Six criteria selected: ❏ Cost ❏ Probability of success ❏ Long-term impact ❏ Provides competitive advantage ❏ Time to implement ❏ Risk of lost sales		
4) Apply criteria and select the three best solutions	Rated solutions against criteria using 1 to 5 scale. Selected:		
	❏ Spend more time determining future plans and needs	Anthony will develop an outline of a "sales planner guide."	May 15
	❏ Develop specific criteria for becoming an "A" or "B" list customer	Larry/Donna will develop a "first pass" at criteria	May 15
	❏ Come up with a training program for customers' employees	Christina/Matt will develop a training outline and talk with customers about it	June 1
5) Next meeting			May 15

The Participant's Role

What if you scheduled a meeting and nobody came? Of course, there would be no meeting. Without Participants, there is no need for a Leader, Facilitator, or Recorder. But a Participant's responsibility is more than just showing up. The success of the meeting depends on the enthusiasm, creativity, commitment, and active participation of every person in attendance. Specifically, Participants:

➟ Know the purpose of the meeting ahead of time

Part of a Participant's job is to know the purpose of the meeting ahead of time in order to prepare for the meeting. The agenda with its stated objective(s) will provide this information. If Participants don't receive an agenda or receive one without a stated objective, they should contact the person who called the meeting. If there's no specific role a Participant is expected to play, then he or she may not need to be there at all!

➟ Confirm attendance

Participants should let the Leader know ahead of time if they can't make it, so the meeting can be rescheduled if necessary, or the Leader can ensure that all those not attending receive a copy of the minutes.

➠ Attend meeting on time

Nothing wastes more time than people strolling into a meeting late. Latecomers either hold up the group by making them wait for everyone to get there, or they show up after the meeting started, causing the group to stop and bring them *"up to speed"* on what's happened so far. In either case, valuable time is being wasted. In some organizations this has become an acceptable habit, and yet the vast majority of people still complain about wasting time in meetings.

➠ Keep an open mind and avoid premature judgment

Meeting Participants need to be prepared to listen to others' opinions, even if they do not agree with them. The key is to be open-minded and not pass judgment on any view until all sides of the issue are taken into consideration.

⟹ Help the Facilitator eliminate distractions and encourage active involvement

Although the Facilitator's role is to deal with distractions, Participants can help. Observations and videotapes of meetings all show something remarkable—that side conversations are contagious! Once one starts, they seem to break out all over the room. Participants should help the Facilitator by not getting dragged into them. They should just say *"no"* to side conversations about sports, the weather, and that new car they've been looking at! There's plenty of time outside the meeting to socialize.

⟹ Share useful ideas

Participants are invited to the meeting to add information, and/or expertise regarding agenda items. They are vital contributors to discussions and group brainstorming sessions. People who attend meetings are called *"Participants"* for a reason!

➠ Support established ground rules and meeting guidelines

The Participants, along with the Facilitator, are responsible for enforcing the ground rules. After all, the ground rules are established to make the meeting more effective and productive. If they are followed, everyone will be able to get the meeting objectives accomplished quickly and move on to more important work.

➠ Help to ensure group consensus

Participants should be focusing on the meeting objective(s). Although there will be different opinions, everyone should be considering how the group can reach an agreement.

Let's see how Penny's group concluded their meeting...

Penny summarized the key decisions and actions made in the meeting, with the assistance of Joe, the Recorder. *"The agenda items we haven't covered can be rolled over to our next meeting,"* she said. Finally, she thanked the Participants for their input during the meeting.

CHAPTER FIVE WORKSHEET:
CONDUCTING YOUR MEETING

Think of the people you've worked with who are the most effective, efficient, organized, and successful meeting Leaders.

1. List examples of things you've observed successful meeting Leaders do that you feel most contributed to an effective meeting, and why.

EXAMPLES	WHY?

2. List examples of things you've observed unsuccessful meeting Leaders do that you feel most contributed to an ineffective meeting, and why.

EXAMPLES	WHY?

3. What are the most common challenges a Facilitator faces in your meetings, and how should they be handled?

FACILITATION CHALLENGES	BEST HANDLED BY

4. When conducting *(or participating)* in your next meeting, what three tips/things do you want to remember?

a.

_____

_____

b.

_____

_____

c.

_____

_____

EVALUATING THE MEETING

In our continual quest to improve, it's the gathering of knowledge that can help build on our human potential. Put into a business context, you need to listen to your customers and determine ways to continually improve how you do your job, in order to keep your customers satisfied.

By viewing the other people in a meeting as customers, the Leader can apply the concepts of customer satisfaction and continuous improvement to help make meetings more effective. That's why the meeting evaluation is an essential component of the meeting process.

It's time to close and evaluate the meeting when...

➠   The meeting objective(s) are met

➠   Additional data is needed before progress
     can be made

➠   The meeting needs the expertise of people not
     present for final decisions

➠   Participants need additional time to assess
     the subject or discuss it with others

➠   Changing events are likely to alter the
     decision

➠   There is not enough time to treat subject
     matter properly

➠   A subgroup or task force can resolve the
     issue more effectively than in the current
     meeting format

➠   Heightened tension inhibits constructive
     progress toward the meeting objective(s)

Participant Evaluation

Following are two types of evaluations. The first is a survey with
statements Participants are asked to rate on a scale of 1 to 5. A
section for comments and suggestions is also provided, so the
Participants can express their opinions.

PARTICIPANT EVALUATION # 1

Leader: _Penny_ **Meeting Date:** _April 20,19XX_

Please rate the degree to which you agree with each statement *(mark appropriate response)*:

	Very Low Degree		Moderate Degree		Very High Degree
1. The Meeting Leader was prepared for the meeting.	1	2	3	4	⑤
2. The Meeting Leader followed the agenda and pushed for accountability.	1	2	3	④	5
3. The Meeting Facilitator encouraged participation from everyone.	1	2	3	4	⑤
4. The Meeting Facilitator monitored time spent on each agenda item.	1	2	3	④	5
5. The Meeting Recorder was prepared for the meeting.	1	2	3	4	⑤
6. The Meeting Recorder regularly checked to ensure appropriate information had been recorded.	1	2	3	4	⑤
7. Meeting Participants were prepared for the meeting.	1	2	3	④	5
8. Meeting Participants had a chance to openly express opinions and ideas.	1	2	3	4	⑤
9. Meeting Participants stayed focused on agenda items.	1	2	3	4	⑤
10. Meeting Participants seemed clear about action item responsibilities.	1	2	3	④	5

Comments/Suggestions:

We still have some people who don't always listen and like to dominate the discussion. We
should do a better job managing these people. They cut the rest of us off too often.

In Participant Evaluation # 1, four of the seven points were rated a five, and the other three criteria scored a four. The comments on the bottom give further improvement suggestions. Using a scale provides a tool to compare one meeting with another, and gives you the advantage of tracking meeting improvement progress.

The second approach is more of an open evaluation that asks Participants to list the positive (+) and negative (-) aspects of the meeting in two separate columns. Again, a section for comments and suggestions is included.

To continually improve...

the way the customer service department held meetings, Paul suggested that the group evaluate its first meeting. *"We need to look at how our team scored and all of our input,"* he said. *"This will give us the opportunity to determine if the meeting process was effective."...*

Here are the results of their Participant Evaluation # 2 form.

PARTICIPANT EVALUATION # 2	
Leader: _Penny_ **Meeting Date:** _April 20,19XX_	
List below *(openly and honestly)* specific examples of what you feel went well (+'s) during this meeting and what didn't go so well (-'s).	
(+'s)	(-'s)
Like being involved Like the ground rules Like sticking to the agenda Like the idea of Facilitator Happy about the solutions Like the selection process	Could have spent less time on this meeting Need to better manage people who dominate the conversation
Additional Suggestions:	
Overall a good meeting. Thanks for asking.	

Participant Evaluation # 2 receives more input from the Participants, as you can see from the comments, and clearly shows what worked well and what needed improvement. It is a particularly useful tool to use when the meeting Participants are willing to take a few minutes to discuss the evaluation, since everyone is already focusing on the pros and cons.

Unfortunately, this *"pluses"* and *"minuses"* type of evaluation doesn't provide a handy set of numbers to compare meetings or track progress, as seen in the first example. Try both and see which one suits your needs. In fact, you may even want to combine both methods.

Now let's look at another type of evaluation, one that the Leader should complete independently after the meeting.

Meeting Leader Self-Evaluation

As a meeting Leader, you have the key responsibility to achieve results and accomplish the objective(s). You also have the responsibility to look at your own performance in leading meetings.

Use the following form to rate the degree to which you agree with each statement describing a particular meeting you regularly lead. Circle the appropriate response on a scale from 1 *(never)* to 5 *(always)*.

		Never		Sometimes		Always
1.	I make sure the meeting is necessary.	1	2	3	4	5
2.	I structure the meeting so that it is appropriate for the meeting purpose and objective(s) *(information, problem solving, decision making, etc.)*.	1	2	3	4	5
3.	I ask the final decision maker to be present during a decision-making meeting.	1	2	3	4	5
4.	I ensure that the appropriate number of key people attend *(those with relevant expertise, affected by the problem, or who need to know the information)*.	1	2	3	4	5
5.	I ensure Participants receive the agenda describing the structure *(content and process)* in advance of the meeting................	1	2	3	4	5
6.	I clearly establish the objectives of the meeting in advance *(so that Participants come with similar expectations)*.	1	2	3	4	5
7.	I ask presenters *(appropriate people responsible for each agenda item)* to be adequately prepared.	1	2	3	4	5
8.	I inform Participants of what to bring and how to prepare.	1	2	3	4	5

		Never		Sometimes		Always
9.	I inform meeting Participants of their roles in advance (*Facilitator, Recorder, Participant, etc.*)..	1	2	3	4	5
10.	When I structure a meeting, I consider the size of the group, the meeting objective, and the action required for each agenda item.	1	2	3	4	5
11.	I make sure the tables and chairs are arranged appropriately (*to support the type of meeting*).	1	2	3	4	5
12.	I ensure the levels of light and heat are adequate, and outside noise that may distract from the meeting is kept to a minimum.	1	2	3	4	5
13.	I make available all required materials and equipment and check that they are functioning properly prior to the meeting.	1	2	3	4	5
14.	I check that all agenda items are appropriate (*clearly written, supportive of the objectives, timed accurately, and sequenced effectively*).	1	2	3	4	5
15.	I ensure that meetings start and end on time.	1	2	3	4	5
16.	I ensure the ground rules, degree of participation required, and agenda objectives are clearly stated.	1	2	3	4	5
17.	During a problem-solving meeting, I clearly state the problem being addressed and propose methods for resolving it.	1	2	3	4	5
18.	During a decision-making meeting, I ask if everyone understands and accepts the decision-making procedures and final authority.	1	2	3	4	5

		Never		Sometimes		Always
19.	I help the group evaluate its progress during the meeting and make necessary changes.	1	2	3	4	5
20.	I make sure that the atmosphere of the meeting is appropriate to the occasion (*formal or informal*).	1	2	3	4	5
21.	In a meeting requiring input, I ask all Participants to contribute (*instead of one or two doing all the talking*).	1	2	3	4	5
22.	I ensure that all agenda items are discussed and closed (*summarized, understanding checked, responsibility assigned, status reports scheduled, etc.*).	1	2	3	4	5
23.	I check that all disruptive behavior (*side conversations, coming in late, personal attacks, etc.*) is managed effectively.	1	2	3	4	5
24.	I summarize the objectives reached and actions to be taken (*including planning the date and agenda for the next meeting*).	1	2	3	4	5
25.	I check to make sure that the minutes are distributed after the meeting (*in a timely manner*).	1	2	3	4	5
26.	I communicate results to those who need to know.	1	2	3	4	5

TOTAL SCORE _____

"To help me improve my team leader meeting skills...

in the future, I am going to complete a Leader's self-evaluation form," said Penny. *"I'm also asking each of you to fill out a Participant's self-evaluation form."...*

Score Interpretation

If your score is between 104-130, there is little evidence that you should be concerned about your ability to lead a productive meeting. If your score is between 78-103, there is some evidence that you should be concerned, particularly if you scored very low on three to five of the items. If your score is between 52-77, you should seriously think about improving your meeting leadership behavior prior to an upcoming meeting. If your score is under 52, then improving your personal meeting behavior should be a top priority!

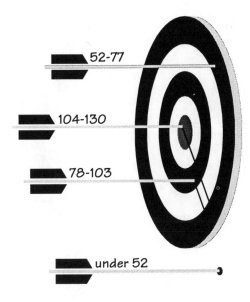

This self-assessment can only be interpreted as a very rough indicator of your readiness to lead productive meetings. The purpose of the assessment is to help you begin the process of identifying meeting leadership behavior that may detract from the effectiveness of meetings you are leading.

Now let's look at a similar evaluation tool for Participants.

Meeting Participant Self-Evaluation

As a meeting Participant consider each of the following statements about your personal meeting involvement. Rate yourself on how well you currently participate in meetings.

Circle the appropriate response on a scale from 1 *(never)* to 5 *(always)* below.

		Never		Sometimes		Always
1.	I make sure I know the purpose of the meeting ahead of time.	1	2	3	4	5
2.	I'm certain of my role in each meeting I attend.	1	2	3	4	5
3.	Prior to a scheduled meeting, I confirm my attendance.	1	2	3	4	5
4.	Prior to attending a meeting, I complete the necessary prework *(e.g., researching information, studying information, etc.).*	1	2	3	4	5
5.	I attend a scheduled meeting on time..........	1	2	3	4	5
6.	During a meeting, I discourage distracting side conversations.	1	2	3	4	5
7.	I do not leave a meeting to handle non-emergency situations/activities.	1	2	3	4	5
8.	If I'm not sure about something discussed in the meeting, I ask questions.	1	2	3	4	5
9.	I'm open to ideas shared by other meeting Participants.	1	2	3	4	5
10.	During a meeting, I'm a good listener.	1	2	3	4	5

		Never	Sometimes	Always
11.	I'm actively involved in open meeting discussions, particularly when I have something meaningful to add.	1 2 3	4	5
12.	If a meeting moves off the agenda, I try to shift the discussion back to the topic at hand.	1 2 3	4	5
13.	I complete the action items to which I've agreed.	1 2 3	4	5
14.	I share my ideas for improving the meeting with the Leader.	1 2 3	4	5
15.	I communicate critical meeting information to those who need to know.	1 2 3	4	5

TOTAL SCORE _____

Score Interpretation

If your score is between 60-75, there is little evidence that you should be concerned about your ability to function as an effective meeting Participant. If your score is between 45-59, there is some evidence that you should be concerned, particularly if you scored very low on three to five of the items. If your score is between 30-44, you should seriously think about improving your personal meeting behavior prior to participating in an upcoming meeting. If your score is under 30, then improving your personal meeting behavior should be a top priority!

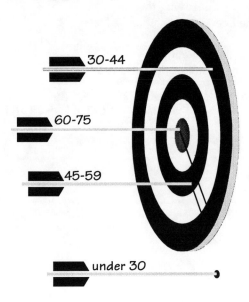

This self-assessment can only be interpreted as a very rough indicator of your readiness to participate effectively in meetings. The purpose of the assessment is to help you begin the process of identifying personal meeting behaviors that may detract from the effectiveness of meetings you attend.

The Facilitator and Recorder of your meetings also have a responsibility to evaluate their performance. Self-evaluations for these two roles are contained in the Appendix.

Later that day Joe and Paul discussed...

the results of the evaluation forms while at the water cooler! *"This is great information,"* Joe said. *"With it, we can plan more productive meetings."*

How often should you evaluate your meetings?

It's important for the Leader to make a judgment call on this. Doing it too often can cause people to lose interest in filling out the form completely and honestly each time.

On the other hand, filling out the forms too infrequently may lead Participants to believe the Leader is just going through the motions and is not interested in their comments.

You be the judge. But remember, it's always good to get a periodic *"maintenance check"* on your meetings, in case they need a *"tune-up."* There's always room for improvement!

CHAPTER SIX WORKSHEET:
EVALUATING YOUR MEETING EFFECTIVELY

1. Based on the pattern of your scores in your Meeting Leader Self-Evaluation, identify below three key issues/concerns about your meetings. Also describe alternative ways to handle them during your upcoming meetings. *(You may wish to discuss these key issues with others, who have participated in meetings with you in the past, to gather additional suggestions.)*

KEY ISSUES/CONCERNS	WAYS TO HANDLE

2. Based on the pattern of your scores in your Meeting Participant Self-Evaluation, identify below three key meeting Participant behaviors you need to improve, and ways to improve them. *(You may wish to discuss these key issues with others who have participated in meetings with you in the past, to gather additional suggestions.)*

MEETING PARTICIPANT BEHAVIORS	WAYS TO IMPROVE

3. What other insights and improvement opportunities have the evaluations presented?

_____

_____

_____

_____

_____

CHAPTER SEVEN

SUMMARY

Most meetings are disorganized and unproductive. They waste time *(that means money)* and result in miscommunication.

So what can you do to stamp out unproductive meeting efforts? You can:

⟹ Identify alternatives to meetings

⟹ Overcome common meeting pitfalls such as problem behavior

⟹ Follow the guidelines for conducting productive meetings

⟹ Learn how to evaluate your meetings

⟹ Implement more proactive meeting plans

Meetings, by their very nature in our complex business world, demand better focus and a more disciplined approach so that you, whether playing the role of a Leader, Facilitator, Recorder, or Participant can see tangible results.

It's Time For A Change

It's time to consider **PREPARING FOR THE MEETING**—the phase where the objective(s) of a meeting are set and items are planned, so the objective(s) can be met. Take the time to plan and coordinate, and you'll create the foundation for a productive, effective meeting.

It's time to consider **CONDUCTING THE MEETING**—the phase where the Leader, Facilitator, Recorder, and Participants combine strong agenda leadership, strong facilitation of group dynamics, and effective recording of information to support the communication effort. They also ensure everyone will stay on the same wavelength and participate.

It's time to consider **EVALUATING THE MEETING**—the phase where the customers *(Participants)* identify problem areas that can be improved by discussing what works and what doesn't work. Evaluate meetings, improve them, and you'll find meetings can really meet your needs.

The Road To More Effective Meetings

As you begin to drive down the
road toward shorter and more
productive meetings, here are a
few final *"driving tips"* to help
make your future meetings more
effective:

➟ Invest time in training and discussing the roles and
responsibilities of the Leader, Facilitator, Recorder and
Participants

➟ Evaluate the new meeting process on a regular basis to
determine its effectiveness over a period of time

➟ Try putting the agenda and meeting minutes into electronic
mail to see if that works better than handing out paper

➟ Keep track of the time and money saved by using the new
meeting process

➟ Send a message of commitment by starting and ending
meetings at the exact designated time

➟ Hang two flip charts at the beginning of every meeting, one
listing the agenda and one with the ground rules

COMMON PROBLEMS AND SOLUTIONS FOR MEETING FACILITATORS

An effective meeting Facilitator remains objective and can handle any given situation. Perhaps the best way to do the work of a Facilitator is to understand why a specific meeting problem exists, and then have several responses available to choose from.

The Facilitator's response should be firm but not controlling or dominating. After all, the Facilitator's first job is to encourage the *"right"* things to happen as well as keep the group on track when necessary, without taking over the meeting process.

Here are some examples of typical problems that come up in meeting situations, why they may exist, and a few possible responses for the Facilitator.

PROBLEM:

SIDE CONVERSATION

A Participant is involved in too many side conversations that are disruptive to the meeting.

Why?

The Participant may:

➡ feel the need to introduce an item totally separate from the original agenda

➡ have a pressing need that makes other agenda items less important

➡ be discussing a topic related to the meeting and feels he or she is not being heard

➡ be bored with the meeting and feel he or she doesn't need to be there

➡ have a need to be the center of attention

Solutions

➤ Ask the Participant: *"If you have an idea, why not share it with the group?"*

➤ Get up and walk around casually near Participants who are having a side conversation. This will usually end their discussion.

➤ Call on the Participant by name and ask: *"Should we add what you are discussing to the agenda?"*

➤ Restate a point recently made in the meeting and ask for his or her opinion.

    Example: *"Sally, we have differing opinions about the new office space layout. What do you think?"*

➤ Suggest to the Participant: *"What you're discussing appears to be very important. Maybe we can set up another meeting to discuss it."*

PROBLEM:

QUIET/SHY PARTICIPANT

A Participant is not participating as you think he or she should.

Why?

The Participant may:

➠ be shy, timid, or insecure

➠ be indifferent to the topic at hand

➠ be bored

➠ feel superior

➠ have no purpose for being at the meeting

➠ not understand the topic(s) being discussed

➠ be distracted by other pressing issues outside the meeting

➠ have personal conflicts with other Participants in the meeting

Solutions

➤ Ask a simple question and make eye contact with this Participant.

➤ Involve the Participant in a small subgroup discussion activity with other Participants.

➤ Ask the Participant to provide the group an oral summary/debriefing of the subgroup discussion.

➤ Recognize his or her contribution immediately and sincerely, and encourage more.

Example: *"Naomi, thanks again for sharing your opinions about the new project. When we start to discuss roles and responsibilities please be sure to let us know what role you'd like to take."*

➤ Inquire during a break or in private about the Participant's own reasons for being so quiet.

➤ Ask a question and suggest that each Participant take a turn sharing their opinion.

Example: *"I'd like to hear from the group, so can we each take a turn sharing a 'pro' and 'con' about the new computer system."*

PROBLEM:

OVERLY TALKATIVE PARTICIPANT

A Participant talks too much, rambles on repeatedly, and is generally dominant.

Why?

The Participant may:

➤ naturally need a lot of attention

➤ have been unprepared for the meeting

➤ have been overly prepared for the meeting

➤ have a great vocabulary and likes to flaunt it

➤ be the person with the most authority *(this is always a tough situation, but it can be managed, without upsetting anyone, using the agenda and the ground rules)*

➤ like to demonstrate that they have extensive knowledge on other subjects

Solutions

➤ Glance at your watch while the Participant is speaking.

➤ Thank the Participant for his or her comments. Then, after he or she stops to take a breath, refocus attention by restating the agenda, the relevant points, and time limits.

    Example: *"Those were some interesting comments, Lois. Now, if we could refocus on agenda item number 3 . . ."*

➤ Ask the Participant to clarify how his or her comments have expanded or added to the discussion at hand.

    Example: *"Kevin, could you help the group understand how the last two points you raised can help us come to a group decision."*

➤ Interject with: *"That's an interesting point. Now let's see what the group thinks of it."*

➤ Remind everyone that there is a time limit on agenda items.

PROBLEM:

OVERLY DISAGREEABLE PARTICIPANT

A Participant is highly argumentative or antagonistic.

Why?

The Participant may:

➠ have a combative personality

➠ be normally good-natured but upset by others' opinions or a specific meeting issue

➠ be the *"show-off"* type and just like to hear him/herself speak

➠ lack the ability to state suggestions constructively

➠ may be antagonized over another issue or feel he or she is being ignored

Solutions

➤ Paraphrase the Participant's comments without using *"loaded"* language. After his or her response to your paraphrasing, recap his or her position in objective terms.

   Example: *"As I understand it, you are suggesting this might cost too much in the long run."*

➤ Find merit in one of the Participant's points; express your agreement *(or get the group to do so)*, then move on.

   Example: *"George, your point about the time it would take to do this is a good one, which we can explore in more detail in a few minutes. Thanks for pointing out your interest in it, and I hope you can give the group some more details a bit later. On the subject of...though..."*

➤ Respond to the content of the Participant's comments, not the attack.

   Example: *"Val, you've raised three points on one side of the issue. Perhaps we can look at them one at a time. As I understand it, your first point is..."*

➤ Throw the Participant's opinions out to the group members, giving them the opportunity to facilitate the argumentative Participant.

   Example: *"Paul, that's an interesting approach to handling this. What do the rest of you think about Paul's idea?"*

➤ Mention that, due to time constraints on the agenda, you may have to table the discussion for now.

TYPES OF MEETINGS

Since you have different objectives for different group meetings, why try to run them all the same way? Meetings are typically most effective when you match the type of meeting you hold with your desired outcomes.

What type of meeting will meet your objectives? Do you only need to inform Participants of a problem, or are you ready to analyze that problem and pick the best solutions?

Your agenda, number of Participants, room arrangement, communication pattern, etc., all need to be consistent with the type of meeting you have chosen to conduct.

Types of Meetings Include...

TYPE	PRIMARY EMPHASIS
Information	Share and discuss important news
Problem Solving	Examine problems, corrections and preventions
Decision Making	Identify criteria and choose alternatives
Team Building	Agree and reinforce common goals
Feedback	Gather input and develop support

The information on the following pages provides you with some basic guidelines and considerations to help you plan your next meeting.

Meeting Type: Information

Examples	⟹ Operations review
	⟹ Project status reports
	⟹ Marketing presentation
	⟹ Staff meeting briefings
Characteristics	⟹ Some opportunity for feedback or questions
	⟹ One-way communication
	⟹ Interaction not encouraged
	⟹ Formal tone
Benefits	⟹ Reinforces Leader's authority
	⟹ Aids understanding of written information
	⟹ Efficient—a lot of information shared
Drawbacks	⟹ One-way not effective if goal is shared responsibility
	⟹ More then 20 minutes of critical information can be lost
Ideal Size	⟹ Four to unlimited
Who Should Attend	⟹ Presenters
	⟹ Those who need to know the information

MEETING TYPE: PROBLEM SOLVING

EXAMPLES	⮕ Deadlines met 60 percent of time?
	⮕ Workload distribution seen as unfair?
	⮕ How to involve top management?
CHARACTERISTICS	⮕ High participation to fully examine problem
	⮕ Clear objectives and right people
	⮕ Supportive climate
BENEFITS	⮕ To collect data for understanding and analysis
	⮕ Shared understanding of problem
	⮕ More divergent ideas
DRAWBACKS	⮕ May only be Leader's problem
	⮕ Problem statements may be inappropriately defined
IDEAL SIZE	⮕ Six to nine people
WHO SHOULD ATTEND	⮕ Appropriate experts
	⮕ Those affected by the problem

MEETING TYPE: DECISION MAKING

EXAMPLES	⟹ Choose the best of three training methods?
	⟹ Which cost-cutting option will meet 15 percent target?
	⟹ Select best media for presentation?
CHARACTERISTICS	⟹ Fully defined problem
	⟹ Objectives and criteria for decision identified
	⟹ Options compared to criteria
BENEFITS	⟹ Participants more informed/ committed
	⟹ Implementation easier if people included in decision
	⟹ Collaboration required for complex decisions
DRAWBACKS	⟹ Overly analytical approach may slow results
	⟹ Quick solutions often only treat symptoms
	⟹ More people means harder to gain consensus
IDEAL SIZE	⟹ Three to six people
WHO SHOULD ATTEND	⟹ Final decision maker
	⟹ Those responsible for implementation

MEETING TYPE: TEAM BUILDING

EXAMPLES	⬌ New project kickoff
	⬌ Cross-functional task force orientation
	⬌ Off-site social event
CHARACTERISTICS	⬌ Agree on common goals, roles, structure
	⬌ Informal tone
	⬌ Climate of trust, sharing and/or fun!
BENEFITS	⬌ Relationships withstand pressures and crises
	⬌ Build appreciation of interdependencies
	⬌ Reduce barriers
DRAWBACKS	⬌ Task-oriented people may see as time waster
	⬌ Requires skill to deal with sensitive issues
	⬌ Too much play, not enough work!
IDEAL SIZE	⬌ Four to unlimited *(break into subgroups if more than twelve members)*
WHO SHOULD ATTEND	⬌ All *"full-time"* members of the team

MEETING TYPE: FEEDBACK

EXAMPLES	⟹ Design review
	⟹ *"Gripe"* session
	⟹ Proposal review
	⟹ Focus Groups
CHARACTERISTICS	⟹ Leader solicits input and options to decide
	⟹ Leader measures *"buy in"* into pre-made decision
BENEFITS	⟹ Ideas, input suggestions, are requested
	⟹ Input is documented
	⟹ *"Buy in"* is enhanced
DRAWBACKS	⟹ Tight structure may prevent valuable input
	⟹ Highly opinionated people may prevent consensus
IDEAL SIZE	⟹ Four to thirty people
WHO SHOULD ATTEND	⟹ Content experts
	⟹ Those potentially affected

REPRODUCIBLE FORMS

MEETING AGENDA

MEETING OBJECTIVE(S):

1. _____

2. _____

3. _____

LOGISTICS:

DATE:

TIME:

LOCATION:

BRING (MATERIALS):

PREPARATION REQUIRED:

GROUP MEMBERS:

1. _____ (LEADER)

2. _____ (FACILITATOR)

3. _____ (RECORDER)

4. _____

5. _____

6. _____

7. _____

8. _____

MEETING CALLED BY: _____

TELEPHONE: _____

AGENDA ITEM	PROCESS	TIME	PERSON(S) RESPONSIBLE

MEETING MINUTES

MEETING OBJECTIVE(S): _____

_____

LEADER: _____   MEETING CALLED BY: _____

FACILITATOR: _____   TIME: FROM _____ TO _____

RECORDER: _____   DATE: _____

MEMBERS PRESENT: MEMBERS ABSENT:

1.   1.

2.   2.

3.   3.

4.   4.

5.   5.

AGENDA ITEM	COMMENTS/ CONCLUSIONS/ ACTIONS (IF ANY)	PERSON(S) RESPONSIBLE	BY WHEN

PARTICIPANT EVALUATION # 1

Leader: _____ **Meeting Date:** _____

Please rate the degree to which you agree with each statement *(mark appropriate response)*:

	Very Low Degree		Moderate Degree		Very High Degree
1. The Meeting Leader was prepared for the meeting.	1	2	3	4	5
2. The Meeting Leader followed the agenda and pushed for accountability.	1	2	3	4	5
3. The Meeting Facilitator encouraged participation from everyone.	1	2	3	4	5
4. The Meeting Facilitator monitored time spent on each agenda item.	1	2	3	4	5
5. The Meeting Recorder was prepared for the meeting.	1	2	3	4	5
6. The Meeting Recorder regularly checked to ensure appropriate information had been recorded.	1	2	3	4	5
7. Meeting Participants were prepared for the meeting.	1	2	3	4	5
8. Meeting Participants had a chance to openly express opinions and ideas.	1	2	3	4	5
9. Meeting Participants stayed focused on agenda items.	1	2	3	4	5
10. Meeting Participants seemed clear about action item responsibilities.	1	2	3	4	5

Comments/Suggestions:

_____

_____

_____

_____

_____

_____

_____

PARTICIPANT EVALUATION # 2

Leader: _____ **Meeting Date:** _____

List below *(openly and honestly)* specific examples of what you feel went well (+'s) during this meeting and what didn't go so well (-'s).

(+'s)	(-'s)

Additional Suggestions:

MEETING LEADER SELF-EVALUATION

As a Meeting Leader, consider each of the following statements about your meeting leadership skills. Rate yourself on how well you currently fulfill the role of Leader in meetings. Circle the appropriate response on a scale from 1 *(never)* to 5 *(always)*.

		Never		Sometimes		Always
1.	I make sure the meeting is necessary.	1	2	3	4	5
2.	I structure the meeting so that it is appropriate for the meeting purpose and objective(s) (*information, problem solving, decision making, etc.*).	1	2	3	4	5
3.	I ask the final decision maker to be present during a decision-making meeting.	1	2	3	4	5
4.	I ensure that the appropriate number of key people attend (*those with relevant expertise, affected by the problem, or who need to know the information*).	1	2	3	4	5
5.	I ensure Participants receive the agenda describing the structure (*content and process*) in advance of the meeting................	1	2	3	4	5
6.	I clearly establish the objectives of the meeting in advance (*so that Participants come with similar expectations*).	1	2	3	4	5
7.	I ask presenters (*appropriate people responsible for each agenda item*) to be adequately prepared.	1	2	3	4	5
8.	I inform Participants of what to bring and how to prepare.	1	2	3	4	5
9.	I inform meeting Participants of their roles in advance (*Facilitator, Recorder, Participant, etc.*)...............................	1	2	3	4	5

	Never		Sometimes		Always

10. When I structure a meeting, I consider the size of the group, the meeting objective, and the action required for each agenda item.   1   2   3   4   5

11. I make sure the tables and chairs are arranged appropriately (*to support the type of meeting*).   1   2   3   4   5

12. I ensure the levels of light and heat are adequate, and outside noise that may distract from the meeting is kept to a minimum.   1   2   3   4   5

13. I make available all required materials and equipment and check that they are functioning properly prior to the meeting.   1   2   3   4   5

14. I check that all agenda items are appropriate (*clearly written, supportive of the objectives, timed accurately, and sequenced effectively*).   1   2   3   4   5

15. I ensure that meetings start and end on time.   1   2   3   4   5

16. I ensure the ground rules, degree of participation required, and agenda objectives are clearly stated.   1   2   3   4   5

17. During a problem-solving meeting, I clearly state the problem being addressed and propose methods for resolving it.   1   2   3   4   5

18. During a decision-making meeting, I ask if everyone understands and accepts the decision-making procedures and final authority.   1   2   3   4   5

19. I help the group evaluate its progress during the meeting and make necessary changes.   1   2   3   4   5

		Never		Sometimes		Always
20.	I make sure that the atmosphere of the meeting is appropriate to the occasion (*formal or informal*).	1	2	3	4	5
21.	In a meeting requiring input, I ask all Participants to contribute (*instead of one or two doing all the talking*).	1	2	3	4	5
22.	I ensure that all agenda items are discussed and closed (*summarized, understanding checked, responsibility assigned, status reports scheduled, etc.*).	1	2	3	4	5
23.	I check that all disruptive behavior (*side conversations, coming in late, personal attacks, etc.*) is managed effectively.	1	2	3	4	5
24.	I summarize the objectives reached and actions to be taken (*including planning the date and agenda for the next meeting*).	1	2	3	4	5
25.	I check to make sure that the minutes are distributed after the meeting (*in a timely manner*).	1	2	3	4	5
26.	I communicate results to those who need to know.	1	2	3	4	5

TOTAL SCORE _____

Score Interpretation

- If your score is between 104-130, there is little evidence that you should be concerned about your ability to lead a productive meeting.

- If your score is between 78-103, there is some evidence that you should be concerned, particularly if you scored very low on three to five of the items.

- If your score is between 52-77, you should seriously think about improving your meeting leadership behavior prior to an upcoming meeting.

- If your score is under 52, improving your personal meeting behavior should probably be a top priority.

MEETING FACILITATOR SELF-EVALUATION

As a Meeting Facilitator, consider each of the following statements about your facilitation skills. Rate yourself on how well you currently fulfill the role of Facilitator in meetings. Circle the appropriate response on a scale from 1 *(never)* to 5 *(always)*.

		Never		Sometimes		Always
1.	I ask questions to draw out quiet Participants.	1	2	3	4	5
2.	I ask questions to challenge the assumptions the group is making.	1	2	3	4	5
3.	Rather than be overly directive, I pose suggestions in the form of questions. For example, I might say, "What would help us to keep focused on the agenda?".............	1	2	3	4	5
4.	I remain neutral during disagreements.	1	2	3	4	5
5.	When a process isn't working very well, I suggest alternative methods.	1	2	3	4	5
6.	I keep the group focused on the issues at hand...	1	2	3	4	5
7.	I monitor the amount of time spent on each agenda item.	1	2	3	4	5
8.	I refocus discussion if Participants have gotten off track.	1	2	3	4	5
9.	I protect people if their ideas are being attacked by other group members.	1	2	3	4	5
10.	I refer to the agreed-upon ground rules when the meeting gets out of hand.	1	2	3	4	5

	Never		Sometimes		Always
11. I manage disruptive behavior effectively (*side conversations, personal attacks, etc.*).	1	2	3	4	5
12. I encourage the Leader to start the meeting on time.	1	2	3	4	5
13. I'm willing to let the Leader know if he/she is monopolizing the discussion.	1	2	3	4	5
14. I coach the Leader, Recorder, and Participants on how to fulfill their roles more effectively.	1	2	3	4	5
15. Prior to attending meetings, I review the agenda.	1	2	3	4	5
16. Before the meeting, I offer to help the Leader with any logistics.	1	2	3	4	5

TOTAL SCORE _____

Score Interpretation

- If your score is between 65-80, there is little evidence that you should be concerned about your ability to function as an effective Meeting Facilitator.
- If your score is between 49-64, there is some evidence that you should be concerned, particularly if you scored very low on three to five of the items.
- If your score is between 33-48, you should seriously think about improving your facilitation skills prior to any upcoming meeting.
- If your score is under 33, improving your meeting facilitation behavior should probably be a top priority.

This assessment can only be interpreted as a very rough indicator of your readiness to facilitate productive meetings. The purpose of the assessment is to help you begin the process of identifying behaviors that may detract from being an effective Facilitator during meetings.

MEETING RECORDER SELF-EVALUATION

As a Meeting Recorder, consider each of the following statements about your recording skills. Rate yourself on how well you currently fulfill the role of Recorder in meetings. Circle the appropriate response on a scale from 1 *(never)* to 5 *(always)*.

		Never		Sometimes		Always
1.	I use a flip chart, whiteboard, or overhead projector to make ideas visible to the participants.	1	2	3	4	5
2.	When using a flip chart, I make sure to print characters that are at least 2-3 inches in size for easy legibility.	1	2	3	4	5
3.	I ask Participants for clarification to make sure that I have the right information.	1	2	3	4	5
4.	I write what others say and avoid adding my own interpretation.	1	2	3	4	5
5.	I write down ideas even if I don't agree with them.	1	2	3	4	5
6.	I focus on writing down only key words and phrases.	1	2	3	4	5
7.	To add clarity, I circle or underline key ideas, decisions, or action items.	1	2	3	4	5
8.	If a lot of data is being generated, I number the charts to maintain the order and flow of information.	1	2	3	4	5
9.	I record meeting minutes on a form that includes a place for action items, person(s) responsible, and due dates.	1	2	3	4	5

	Never		Sometimes		Always
10. I make an effort to distribute the meeting minutes immediately after the meeting.	1	2	3	4	5
11. If necessary, I ask Participants to repeat their ideas and comments in order to record them accurately.	1	2	3	4	5
12. I use a variety of colored markers with flip charts to add clarity and to highlight main points.	1	2	3	4	5
13. I try to write as quickly as possible, while maintaining legibility.	1	2	3	4	5
14. When in the role of Recorder, I also make contributions as a team member.	1	2	3	4	5
15. I summarize often during a meeting to make sure that I've accurately captured everyone's ideas and comments.	1	2	3	4	5

TOTAL SCORE _____

Score Interpretation

- If your score is between 60-75, there is little evidence that you should be concerned about your ability to function as an effective Meeting Recorder.
- If your score is between 45-59, there is some evidence that you should be concerned, particularly if you scored very low on three to five of the items.
- If your score is between 30-44, you should seriously think about improving your Recorder skills prior to any upcoming meeting.
- If your score is under 30, improving your Meeting Recorder behaviors should probably be a top priority.

This assessment can only be interpreted as a very rough indicator of your readiness to effectively record meetings. The purpose of the assessment is to help you begin the process of identifying behaviors that may detract from being an effective Recorder during meetings.

MEETING PARTICIPANT SELF-EVALUATION

As a meeting Participant, consider each of the following statements about your personal meeting involvement. Rate yourself on how well you currently participate in meetings. Circle the appropriate response on a scale from 1 *(never)* to 5 *(always)*.

		Never		Sometimes		Always
1.	I make sure I know the purpose of the meeting ahead of time.	1	2	3	4	5
2.	I'm certain of my role in each meeting I attend.	1	2	3	4	5
3.	Prior to a scheduled meeting, I confirm my attendance.	1	2	3	4	5
4.	Prior to attending a meeting, I complete the necessary prework *(e.g., researching information, studying information, etc.)*.	1	2	3	4	5
5.	I attend a scheduled meeting on time..........	1	2	3	4	5
6.	During a meeting, I discourage distracting side conversations.	1	2	3	4	5
7.	I do not leave a meeting to handle non-emergency situations/activities.	1	2	3	4	5
8.	If I'm not sure about something discussed in the meeting, I ask questions.	1	2	3	4	5
9.	I'm open to ideas shared by other meeting Participants.	1	2	3	4	5
10.	During a meeting, I'm a good listener.	1	2	3	4	5

	Never	Sometimes	Always

11. I'm actively involved in open meeting
    discussions, particularly when I have
    something meaningful to add. 1   2   3   4   5

12. If a meeting moves off the agenda, I try
    to shift the discussion back to the topic
    at hand. 1   2   3   4   5

13. I complete the action items to which
    I've agreed. 1   2   3   4   5

14. I share my ideas for improving the
    meeting with the Leader. 1   2   3   4   5

15. I communicate critical meeting
    information to those who need to know. 1   2   3   4   5

TOTAL SCORE _____

Score Interpretation

- If your score is between 60-75, there is little evidence that you should be concerned about your ability to function as an effective meeting Participant.

- If your score is between 45-59, there is some evidence that you should be concerned, particularly if you scored very low on three to five of the items.

- If your score is between 30-44, you should seriously think about improving your personal meeting behavior prior to participating in an upcoming meeting.

- If your score is under 30, improving your personal meeting behavior should probably be a top priority.

This assessment can only be interpreted as a very rough indicator of your readiness to effectively participate in meetings. The purpose of the assessment is to help you begin the process of identifying behaviors that may detract from being an effective Participant during meetings.

Professional And Personal Development Publications From Richard Chang Associates, Inc.

Designed to support continuous learning, these highly targeted, integrated collections from Richard Chang Associates, Inc. (RCA) help individuals and organizations acquire the knowledge and skills needed to succeed in today's ever-changing workplace. Titles are available through RCA, Jossey-Bass, Inc., fine bookstores, and distributors internationally.

Practical Guidebook Collection

Quality Improvement Series

Continuous Process Improvement
Continuous Improvement Tools, Volume 1
Continuous Improvement Tools, Volume 2
Step-By-Step Problem Solving
Meetings That Work!
Improving Through Benchmarking
Succeeding As A Self-Managed Team
Measuring Organizational Improvement Impact
Process Reengineering In Action
Satisfying Internal Customers First!

Management Skills Series

Interviewing And Selecting High Performers
On-The-Job Orientation And Training
Coaching Through Effective Feedback
Expanding Leadership Impact
Mastering Change Management
Re-Creating Teams During Transitions
Planning Successful Employee Performance
Coaching For Peak Employee Performance
Evaluating Employee Performance

High Performance Team Series

Success Through Teamwork
Building A Dynamic Team
Measuring Team Performance
Team Decision-Making Techniques

High-Impact Training Series

Creating High-Impact Training
Identifying Targeted Training Needs
Mapping A Winning Training Approach
Producing High-Impact Learning Tools
Applying Successful Training Techniques
Measuring The Impact Of Training
Make Your Training Results Last

Workplace Diversity Series

Capitalizing On Workplace Diversity
Successful Staffing In A Diverse Workplace
Team Building For Diverse Work Groups
Communicating In A Diverse Workplace
Tools For Valuing Diversity

Personal Growth And Development Collection

Managing Your Career in a Changing Workplace
Unlocking Your Career Potential
Marketing Yourself and Your Career
Making Career Transitions
Memory Tips For The Forgetful

101 Stupid Things Collection

101 Stupid Things Trainers Do To Sabotage Success
101 Stupid Things Supervisors Do To Sabotage Success
101 Stupid Things Employees Do To Sabotage Success
101 Stupid Things Salespeople Do To Sabotage Success
101 Stupid Things Business Travelers Do To Sabotage Success

ABOUT RICHARD CHANG ASSOCIATES, INC.

Richard Chang Associates, Inc. (RCA) is a multi-disciplinary organizational performance improvement firm. Since 1987, RCA has provided private and public sector clients around the world with the experience, expertise, and resources needed to build capability in such critical areas as process improvement, management development, project management, team performance, performance measurement, and facilitator training. RCA's comprehensive package of services, products, and publications reflect the firm's commitment to practical, innovative approaches and to the achievement of significant, measurable results.

RCA RESOURCES OPTIMIZE ORGANIZATIONAL PERFORMANCE

CONSULTING — Using a broad range of skills, knowledge, and tools, RCA consultants assist clients in developing and implementing a wide range of performance improvement initiatives.

TRAINING — Practical, "real world" training programs are designed with a "take initiative" emphasis. Options include off-the-shelf programs, customized programs, and public and on-site seminars.

CURRICULUM AND MATERIALS DEVELOPMENT — A cost-effective and flexible alternative to internal staffing, RCA can custom-develop and/or customize content to meet both organizational objectives and specific program needs.

VIDEO PRODUCTION — RCA's award-winning, custom video productions provide employees with information in a consistent manner that achieves lasting impact.

PUBLICATIONS — The comprehensive and practical collection of publications from RCA supports organizational training initiatives and self-directed learning.

PACKAGED PROGRAMS — Designed for first-time and experienced trainers alike, these programs offer comprehensive, integrated materials (including selected Practical Guidebooks) that provide a wide range of flexible training options. Choose from:

- Meetings That Work! ToolPAK™
- Step-By-Step Problem Solving ToolKIT™
- Continuous Process Improvement Packaged Training Program
- Continuous Improvement Tools, Volume 1 ToolPAK™
- Continuous Improvement Tools, Volume 2 ToolPAK™
- High Involvement Teamwork™ Packaged Training Program

RICHARD
CHANG
ASSOCIATES

World Class Resources. World Class Results.℠

Richard Chang Associates, Inc.

Corporate Headquarters

15265 Alton Parkway, Suite 300, Irvine, California 92618 USA

(800) 756-8096 • (949) 727-7477 • Fax: (949) 727-7007

E-Mail: info@rca4results.com • www.richardchangassociates.com

U.S. Offices in Irvine and Atlanta • Licensees and Distributors Worldwide